Early TRANSPORTATION Encyclopedias

PLANES

by Priyanka Lamichhane

Early Encyclopedias

An Imprint of Abdo Reference
abdobooks.com

abdobooks.com

Published by Abdo Reference, a division of ABDO, PO Box 398166, Minneapolis, Minnesota 55439.
Copyright © 2024 by Abdo Consulting Group, Inc. International copyrights reserved in all countries.
No part of this book may be reproduced in any form without written permission from the
publisher. Early Encyclopedias™ is a trademark and logo of Abdo Reference.
Printed in China

THIS BOOK CONTAINS
RECYCLED MATERIALS

102023
012024

Editor: Carrie Hasler
Series Designer: Candice Keimig

Library of Congress Control Number: 2023939677

Publisher's Cataloging-in-Publication Data

Names: Lamichhane, Priyanka, author.
Title: Planes / by Priyanka Lamichhane
Description: Minneapolis, Minnesota : Abdo Reference, 2024 | Series: Early transportation
    encyclopedias | Includes online resources and index.
Identifiers: ISBN 9781098292935 (lib. bdg.) | ISBN 9798384910879 (ebook)
Subjects: LCSH: Airplanes--Juvenile literature. | Aviation--Juvenile literature. | Planes (Airplanes)--
    Juvenile literature. | Airplanes--History--Juvenile literature. | Vehicles--Juvenile literature. |
    Transportation--Juvenile literature. | Encyclopedias and dictionaries--Juvenile literature.
Classification: DDC 629.224--dc23

CONTENTS

Welcome Aboard!

It is fun to look up and see an airplane! People have always dreamed of flying. Many have tried to find a way to fly for a very long time. The first airplane was invented in 1903. Orville and Wilbur Wright built it in North Carolina. After that, airplanes took off!

Some planes carry people. Other planes take things from here to there. These trucks in the sky are called cargo planes. Have you heard of seaplanes? They land on water. Some planes help people work from the sky. There are planes that help the military too. There are even planes that do tricks. There is much to discover about planes!

How Planes Fly

Planes fly using something called lift. Lift is created with the help of the wings and with speed. The plane speeds down the runway. Air flows over the top of the wings. The plane lifts off the ground. It is flying!

Lift is stronger than gravity. Gravity is the force that pulls everything down to Earth. Engines help a plane fly too. They push the plane forward in the air.

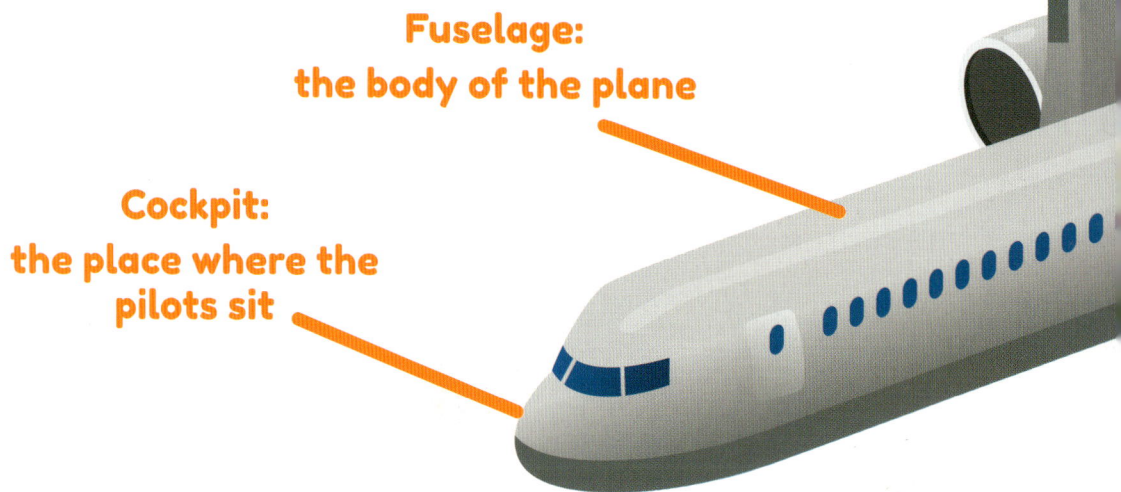

Fuselage:
the body of the plane

Cockpit:
the place where the pilots sit

Parts of a Plane

These are the main parts of a plane. Take a look!

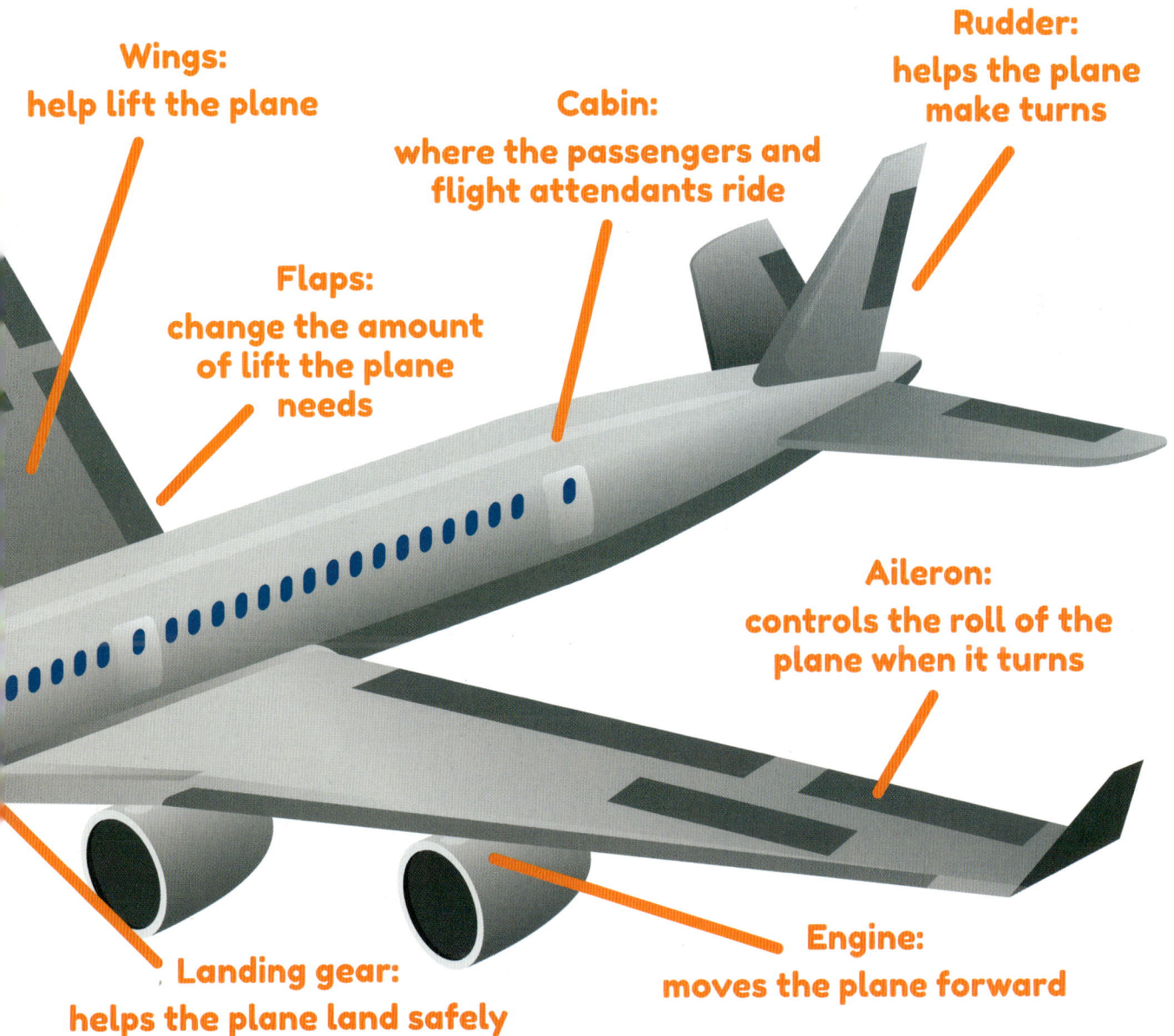

Wings:
help lift the plane

Cabin:
where the passengers and
flight attendants ride

Rudder:
helps the plane
make turns

Flaps:
change the amount
of lift the plane
needs

Aileron:
controls the roll of the
plane when it turns

Landing gear:
helps the plane land safely

Engine:
moves the plane forward

1903: The Wright brothers built the first airplane.

1914: World War I was the first time airplanes were used in a war in large numbers.

1927: Charles Lindbergh became the first person to fly alone across the Atlantic Ocean.

1932: Amelia Earhart became the first woman to fly alone across the Atlantic Ocean.

1939: Pan American Airways began flying across the Atlantic Ocean.

1969: The Boeing 747 was the first jumbo jet passenger airplane.

1973: The superfast Concorde made its first trip across the Atlantic Ocean in less than four hours.

1996: Airbus began making plans to build a jumbo airplane.

2008: Biofuel was used to power a passenger flight. Biofuel is made from plants like corn.

2022: The first all-electric plane took flight.

Blériot XI Monoplane

The Blériot XI monoplane was built in France in 1909. It only had room for one person. The plane was made of wood. It was not as fast as planes today. It could fly 47 miles per hour (76 kmh). Most cars today travel faster than that!

In July 1909, it was the first plane to fly across the English Channel. This is the body of water between England and France. The flight took 37 minutes.

FUN FACT!

The Blériot XI is named after its inventor, Louis Blériot.

Size:
23 feet long
(7 m)

How Far:
50 miles
(80 km)

How High:
3,218 feet
(981 m)

How Fast:
47 miles per hour
(76 kmh)

Curtiss JN-4H

Airplanes help us send mail. Mail can get to faraway places faster. The US Post Office started using planes in 1918. The first plane they used was the Curtiss JN-4H. It was nicknamed the "Jenny."

The post office started with six planes. They first flew between Washington, DC, New York City, and Philadelphia. By 1924, planes were taking mail all over the country. This little plane could carry 300 pounds (136 kg) of mail at a time.

Size:
27 feet
(8 m)

How Far:
175 miles
(282 kmh)

How High:
11,000 feet
(3,353 m)

How Fast:
80 mph
(129 kmh)

FUN FACT!

Carrier pigeons were used to carry mail during World War II.

Ford Tri-Motor

The Ford Tri-Motor was made of metal. It was called the Tin Goose. The plane flew for the first time in 1926. It was one of the first planes to carry people. The first Tri-Motor carried eight people. Later ones carried 17 people.

Size:	How High:	How Far:	How Fast:
50 feet long (15 m)	18,000 feet (5,486 m)	572 miles (921 km)	140 mph (225 kmh)

This plane was made by the Ford Motor Company. The company started by making cars. Ford still makes cars today. It does not make planes anymore.

Lockheed 10-E Electra

The Lockheed 10-E Electra was Amelia Earhart's plane. In 1932, Amelia was the first woman to fly alone across the Atlantic Ocean. Later that year she became the first woman to fly across the United States.

Size:
39 feet long
(12 m)

How High:
19,400 feet
(5,913 m)

How Far:
713 miles
(1,147 km)

How Fast:
202 mph
(325 kmh)

In 1936, Amelia bought a Lockheed 10-E Electra airplane. She wanted to fly it around the world. For this flight, it was just Amelia and a navigator named Fred Noonan. They flew to lots of places, but they got lost. No one has ever found them.

FUN FACT!

Today, a copy of Amelia's plane is in a museum in her home state of Kansas.

Spirit of St. Louis

The Spirit of St. Louis flew across the Atlantic Ocean in May 1927. It was the first plane to do so. Pilot Charles Lindbergh traveled from New York to France.

Size:
28 feet long
(9 m)

How Far:
4,100 miles
(6,598 km)

How High:
10,000 feet
(3,048 m)

How Fast:
120 mph
(193 kmh)

Did You Know?

The Spirit of St. Louis is now at the National Air and Space Museum in Washington, DC.

He had to fly through cold weather and fog. It took him more than 33 hours! A big crowd was waiting to see him when he landed.

FUN FACT!

There was a big parade in New York City after Lindbergh's flight.

Wright Flyers (I, II, III)

Wilbur and Orville Wright were brothers from Ohio. They were the first people to get an airplane to fly. The brothers were interested in flying from a young age. As children, they played with toy helicopters.

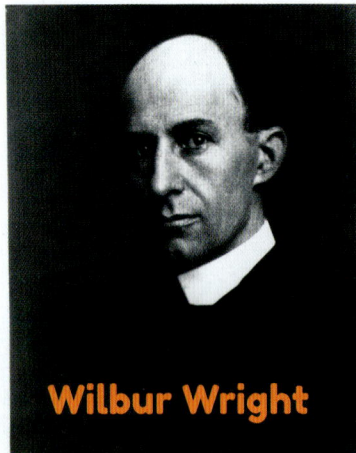

Wilbur Wright

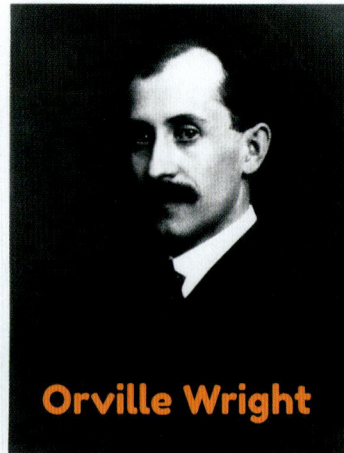

Orville Wright

Size:
21 feet long
(6 m)

How High:
10 feet
(3 m)

How Far:
852 feet
(260 m)

How Fast:
30 to 31 mph
(48 to 50 kmh)

In 1903, the brothers created the Wright Flyer I plane. It took off in Kitty Hawk, North Carolina. It flew for 12 seconds. There were no seats on the plane. Only the pilot could fit. The pilot had to lie down in the front. It was the first plane that was powered by an engine.

FUN FACT!

Before building airplanes, the Wright brothers made bicycles.

The Wright brothers made another plane in 1904. It was called the Wright Flyer II. It was the first plane to fly in a circle. It flew for 3 miles (5 km). That took five minutes.

FUN FACT!

The Wright Flyers helped other people learn how to build planes.

In 1905, the brothers made the Wright Flyer III. It flew longer and better than the first two. Later, the brothers made the first plane that could carry two people. They called it Model A.

Did You Know?

The Wright brothers' first flying machine was actually a large kite. The kite helped them learn how to build better wings.

Aero Spacelines Super Guppy

The Super Guppy was really BIG! It carried rocket parts across the country for NASA. The Super Guppy was built in 1965. Before that, rocket parts had to be moved by ship. It took a long time. There were no planes that could fit the parts.

This plane looked like a big balloon. The front of the plane opened up so rocket parts could go inside. NASA used the first Super Guppy until 1991. Other Super Guppy planes were built after that. There is only one left today.

Size:
144 feet long
(44 m)

How High:
25,000 feet
(7,620 m)

How Far:
2,000 miles
(3,219 km)

How Fast:
250 mph
(402 kmh)

Antonov An-225 Mriya

The Antonov is the largest plane in the world. This plane needed to be extra large. Why? It was made to carry something really big—a space shuttle! But the shuttle did not go inside. The shuttle rode on the plane's back. It was like an airplane piggyback ride!

The Antonov has 32 wheels and six engines. They are needed for liftoff. It also has 13 fuel tanks that sit inside the wings.

Size:
275 feet long
(84 m)

How Far:
9,600 miles
(15,450 km)

How High:
36,000 feet
(10,973 m)

How Fast:
528 mph
(850 kmh)

FUN FACT!

The Antonov was built to carry the Russian Buran space shuttle.

The Antonov has two levels. The top floor is where people ride. In the front is the cockpit where the pilots sit. Only the pilots can see outside. There are no windows anywhere else. There are also two cabins. One is where people can sit and work. The other cabin is for resting.

The bottom floor holds all the cargo. It carries many different things. In order to carry heavy loads and have two floors, the Antonov was made to be very tall. In fact, it is about as tall as a six-story building!

Beluga XL

The Beluga XL airplane is named for a beluga whale. And it's easy to see why. It is white with a round head. It even has a face!

The "head" of the Beluga XL airplane opens really wide. This makes it easy to load large items. The Beluga XL carries large parts for other airplanes. It also moves cargo like helicopters. The airplane is so big that it has three levels.

Size:
207 feet long
(63 m)

How Far:
2,485 miles
(3,999 km)

How High:
35,000 feet
(10,668 m)

How Fast:
529 mph
(851 kmh)

FUN FACT!

The Beluga XL flies more than 4 million miles per year. That's the same as about 17 trips to the moon!

DELIVERY SERVICE PLANES

Delivery Service Planes help us by taking packages from one place to another. On the outside, these planes look like the planes people ride. But delivery planes look different on the inside. There are no seats. The middle of the plane is a big open space. It is called the cargo hold.

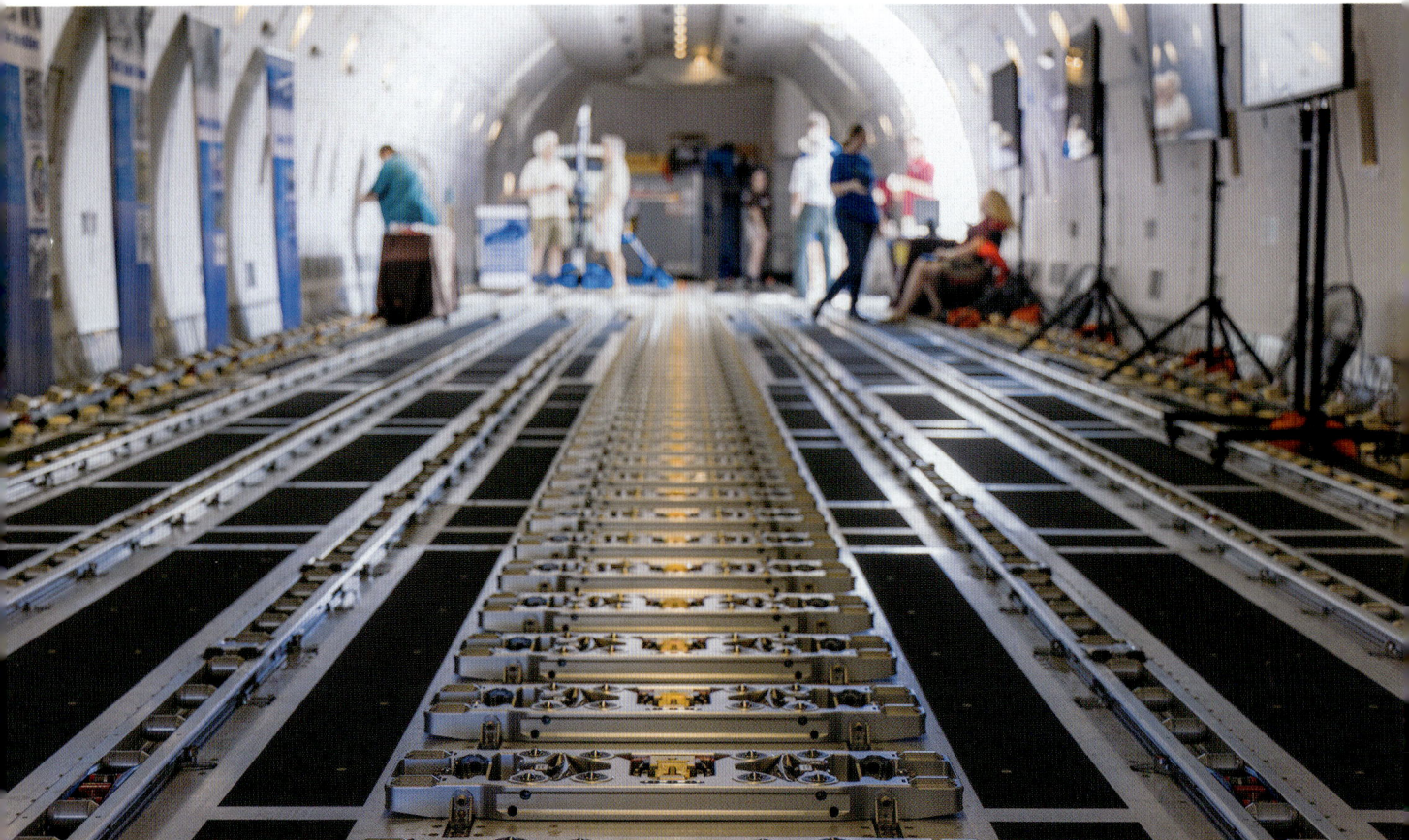

The cargo hold is filled with lots of boxes. The boxes cannot go just anywhere. They have to be put in certain places. Why? To make sure the plane is balanced. The weight on a plane has to be even so it can fly.

Boeing 747-8F

The Boeing 747-8F is one of the biggest delivery planes. The nose of the plane opens up to load extra-large cargo.

Size:
250 feet long
(76 m)

How Far:
8,960 miles
(14,420 km)

How High:
42,100 feet
(12,832 m)

How Fast:
660 miles per hour
(1,062 kmh)

DELIVERY SERVICE PLANES

A cargo plane has just two people on board—the pilots! But if the flight is more than eight hours long, three or four pilots will be on board. That way, the pilots can take turns flying.

Cars and trucks deliver cargo to the airport. A special lift then moves the cargo up and into the plane.

A-10 Thunderbolt II

This fighter plane was made for the US Air Force. It helps troops, or soldiers, in the field. There is only enough room for one pilot.

Size:
53 feet long
(16 m)

How High:
45,000 feet
(13,716 m)

How Far:
2,580 miles
(4,152 km)

How Fast:
518 mph
(834 kmh)

The plane carries military weapons. The weapons are used when there is fighting and troops need help. This plane gets close to the ground to make an attack. It can even shoot from its nose. Since it needs to fly low, it moves slower than other planes. But it moves easily. The plane can quickly fly in, make an attack, and fly out.

FUN FACT!

The A-10 Thunderbolt II is nicknamed the "Warthog."

B-2 Spirit

The B-2 Spirit is a stealth bomber. It can fly without being seen, even by radar systems. Radar uses invisible waves to find things. It can find things that are far away or hidden. A radar system sends out waves. When the waves hit an object, they bounce back.

FUN FACT!

The B-2 Spirit has appeared in lots of Hollywood movies.

But radar can't find the B-2 Spirit! The plane is covered in a special material that helps hide it from radar. Robots spray the material on the plane before it flies.

Did You Know?

Bats and dolphins can find things using invisible waves too. This special ability is called echolocation.

Size:
69 feet long
(21 m)

How High:
50,000 feet
(15,240 m)

How Far:
6,900 miles
(11,104 km)

How Fast:
628 mph
(1,011 kmh)

C-17 Globemaster III

This plane carries cargo and troops around the world. It also drops them from the air! The troops use parachutes to float to the ground. When it is time to jump, a door opens on the side of the plane. Sometimes people jump from a large back door.

The C-17 also drops military tanks. It is the only airplane that can drop such large cargo. It is called an airdrop. The tanks slide out from a large back door. When the door is open, it looks like a big ramp.

FUN FACT!

Troops that jump out of airplanes are called paratroopers.

Size:
174 feet long
(53 m)

How High:
45,000 feet
(13,716 m)

How Far:
2,785 miles
(4,482 km)

How Fast:
570 mph
(917 kmh)

Curtiss P-40 Warhawk

The Warhawk was used during World War II. More than 13,000 were built for the war. They were used by 28 different countries. The Warhawk flew with a propeller on the front. The Warhawk carried just one person, the pilot.

Size:
31 feet long
(9 m)

How High:
30,000 feet
(9,144 m)

How Far:
850 miles
(1,368 km)

How Fast:
362 mph
(583 kmh)

A group of pilots who flew this plane were called the Flying Tigers. Why? The noses of their planes were painted with rows of teeth.

F-16 Fighting Falcon

The Fighting Falcon is fast! It makes a loud sound called a sonic boom. A sonic boom makes waves in the air. These are called shock waves. The waves happen because the plane flies faster than sound can travel.

The F-16 is not only fast. It has lots of moves. It can spin in circles. It can even dive, just like a peregrine falcon. The military uses this plane to fight other planes. It can also help with attacks on the ground.

Size:
49 feet long
(15 m)

How Far:
2,000 miles
(3,219 km)

How High:
50,000 feet
(15,240 m)

How Fast:
1,500 mph
(2,414 kmh)

Did You Know?

The F-16 cockpit has a clear cover. It is called a bubble canopy. It gives the pilot full views of everything.

KC-46A Pegasus Tanker

The KC-46A Pegasus Tanker is a gas station in the air! It can fuel military planes while they're flying. When a plane needs fuel, it flies just below the tanker. Jet fuel is stored in tanks. A hose, called a boom, comes out from the back of the tanker. The boom attaches to the plane. Then fuel goes through. Fill 'er up!

Size:
159 feet long
(48 m)

How High:
40,000 feet
(12,192 m)

How Far:
7,158 miles
(11,520 km)

How Fast:
529 mph
(851 kmh)

Did You Know?

Once the boom is connected, fuel goes through at 1,200 gallons per minute (4,542 liters per minute). That's enough liquid to fill about 15 bathtubs!

Did You Know?
The C-5M Galaxy can carry up to 15 Humvees!

Lockheed C-5M Super Galaxy

The C-5M is the US Air Force's biggest plane. The plane carries helicopters and tanks. It carries lots of other cargo too.

The nose of the C-5M opens wide. This way, big vehicles can roll in. There are ramps at both ends of the plane. Having two places to load cargo helps get items on and off fast.

Size:
247 feet long
(75 m)

How Far:
5,500 miles
(8,851 km)

How High:
33,000 feet
(10,058 m)

How Fast:
518 mph
(834 kmh)

FUN FACT!

The C-5M has 28 wheels. It needs them to hold a lot of weight.

Mitsubishi Zero

The Mitsubishi Zero flew during World War II. It was Japan's best plane. It was lighter than other planes. It could move quickly and easily, making twists and turns in the air.

The Zero had a special trick. It had two fuel tanks—one on the inside and one on the outside. When the outside fuel tank was empty, it dropped off the plane. This helped the Zero stay light so it could fly longer.

Size:
30 feet long
(9 m)

How Far:
1,900 miles
(3,058 km)

How High:
38,500 feet
(11,735 m)

How Fast:
350 mph
(563 kmh)

FUN FACT!

Each Mitsubishi Zero had four red dots painted on its body. This made the plane stand out.

North American X-15

The North American X-15 moved at lightning speed. The plane was made to fly high and fast. It flew so high that it touched space! Scientists used this plane to learn how to make spaceships.

Size:
50 feet long
(15 m)

How Fast:
4,500 mph
(7,242 kmh)

How High:
It reached space!

How Far:
This plane only flew for about 10 minutes at a time.

Did You Know?

Neil Armstrong was one of the X-15 pilots. He later became the first person to walk on the moon.

Most planes take off from the ground. The X-15 took off from the air! It sat under the wing of a large plane called the B-52 Mothership. Once the B-52 reached 45,000 feet (13,716 m), the X-15 came off the wing and blasted high into the clouds.

P-51 Mustang

P-51 Mustangs were fighter planes. They flew during World War II and carried weapons. These planes were very colorful. Some had stars. Some had stripes.

FUN FACT!

The planes had special cameras that could take pictures from above.

Like some planes today, P-51 Mustangs had a clear bubble over the cockpit. The pilots could see all around. This plane also had an extra job. Some were used as spy planes to watch the enemy.

Size:
32 feet long
(10 m)

How Far:
1,375 miles
(2,213 km)

How High:
41,900 feet
(12,771 m)

How Fast:
390 miles per hour
(628 kmh)

A special group of P-51 Mustangs had red tails. These belonged to a group called the Tuskegee Airmen. They were the first African American US military pilots. They were trained at the Tuskegee Airbase in Alabama.

Did You Know?

Model airplanes are small planes you can build yourself. The Mustang is a popular choice for many model airplane builders. Model airplane kits became popular after World War II.

The airmen flew
the planes many times during
the war. Part of their job was
to protect military bombers.
The airmen flew alongside the
bombers. They attacked any
enemy planes that tried to hit
the bombers.

Sopwith Camel

The Sopwith Camel played a big part in World War I. It was a fighter plane. But it was hard to fly. The pilots had to be well trained. The plane was small. It had just enough room for the pilot.

Did You Know?

Each plane had a red, white, and blue circle painted on the side and on the top wing. The tail was red, white, and blue too.

The Camel was built in Great Britain. Weapons were attached to the top in front of the pilot's seat. They were hidden with a cover. This cover made the plane look like it had a hump. That is how the Camel got its name.

FUN FACT!

There were more than 5,000 Sopwith Camels built during World War I.

Size:
19 feet long
(6 m)

How Far:
300 miles
(483 km)

How High:
19,000 feet
(5,791 m)

How Fast:
117 mph
(188 kmh)

SR-71 Blackbird

The Blackbird was a spy plane. It was built in secret in the 1950s. It took a few years to get it right.

In 1964, President Lyndon B. Johnson told people about the plane. He said the Blackbird had made its first flight and it was very fast! How fast? At takeoff, it flew more than 200 miles per hour (322 kmh). After takeoff, it got even faster.

Size:
107 feet long
(33 m)

How Far:
2,900 miles
(4,667 km)

How High:
85,000 feet
(25,908 m)

How Fast:
2,200 mph
(3,541 kmh)

Did You Know?
When the Blackbird was in the air, it gathered information about things that were happening on the ground. In one hour, it could gather information from an area the size of Wyoming.

The Blackbird got its name from the black paint that covered it. This paint was special. It had three jobs. It made sure the Blackbird could not be found by radar.

The paint also stopped the plane from catching on fire. The Blackbird was so fast that its engines got hot. Without the special paint, the plane might have burned.

The paint also hid the plane in the dark. You could not see it against a black sky.

FUN FACT!

The Blackbird's last flight was from Los Angeles to Washington, DC. It took just a little over one hour!

Super Hornet F/A-18F

Super Hornets take off and land on ships called aircraft carriers. These military planes do a lot of jobs.

They can act as spy planes. They can protect and refuel other planes in the air. They can also strike enemies on the ground or on the water.

Size:
60 feet long
(18 m)

How High:
50,000 feet
(15,240 m)

How Far:
1,467 miles
(2,361 km)

How Fast:
1,200 mph
(1,931 kmh)

FUN FACT!

The Super Hornet was in the 2022 movie *Top Gun: Maverick.*

The Blue Angels are a special group of navy and marine corps pilots. They travel around the country. They perform aerobatics in air shows.

The Blue Angels use Super Hornets to swirl, dip, and dive in the sky. The skilled pilots have to train for a long time.

One of their most popular moves is called a formation. This is when a few planes come together in a special shape in the sky.

FUN FACT!

The Blue Angels have been around for almost 80 years!

XB-70 Valkyrie

The Valkyrie was a fast bomber. But it never flew in battle. When it was being tested, the plane did not go as fast as it was supposed to. It was also a little too bumpy. The military decided not to make anymore.

Instead, the air force made the Valkyrie a test plane. They wanted to see how well it would fly using some new technology.

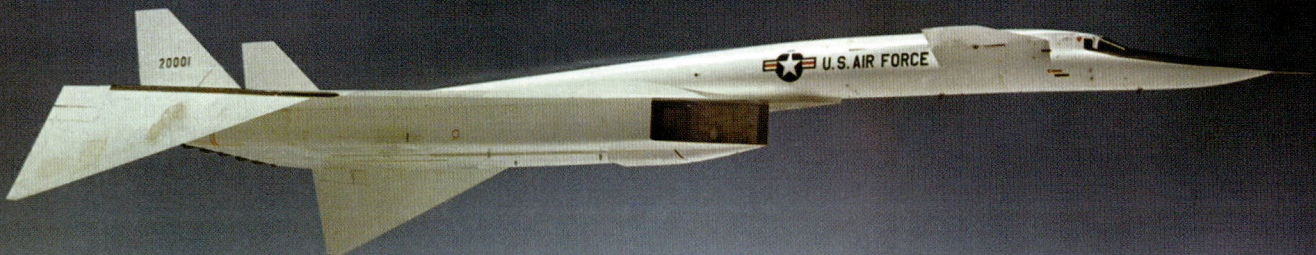

Size:
192 feet long
(59 m)

How Far:
4,300 miles
(6,920 km)

How High:
77,350 feet
(23,576 m)

How Fast:
2,056 mph
(3,309 kmh)

All of these tests gave the air force good information. They used the information to help make other planes.

Airbus

Airbus passenger planes take people all over the world. Airbus has a lot of airplanes. Some are really big. Some are small. Airbus planes can carry 100 to 850 people. Their smallest passenger plane is called the A220. The biggest is the Airbus A380. It is the biggest passenger plane ever built. It is also known as a jumbo jet.

Airbus A380

Size:
240 feet long
(73 m)

How High:
43,000 feet
(13,106 m)

How Far:
9,320 miles
(14,999 km)

How Fast:
683 mph
(1,099 kmh)

The Airbus A350 is another popular plane. This plane fits 350 people. It makes some long flights.

One airline is taking the A350 very far. Qantas is Australia's main airline. It plans to fly the A350 for 19 hours. It will go from Sydney to New York City with no stops!

FUN FACT!

Airbus also makes helicopters.

The smaller A220 airplane is used for shorter flights. These planes are easier to land in airports that are near big cities where there are lots of buildings close together.

Airbus A220

Size:
115 feet long
(35 m)

How High:
40,000 feet
(12,192 m)

How Far:
2,531 miles
(4,073 km)

How Fast:
541 mph
(871 kmh)

Air Force One

Air Force One is the president's plane! It is a Boeing 747. But the inside does not look like other planes. There are rooms inside! The president has an office. There is a bedroom for sleeping. There is a bathroom, and it has a shower too!

FUN FACT!

Franklin Roosevelt was the first sitting president to fly in an airplane.

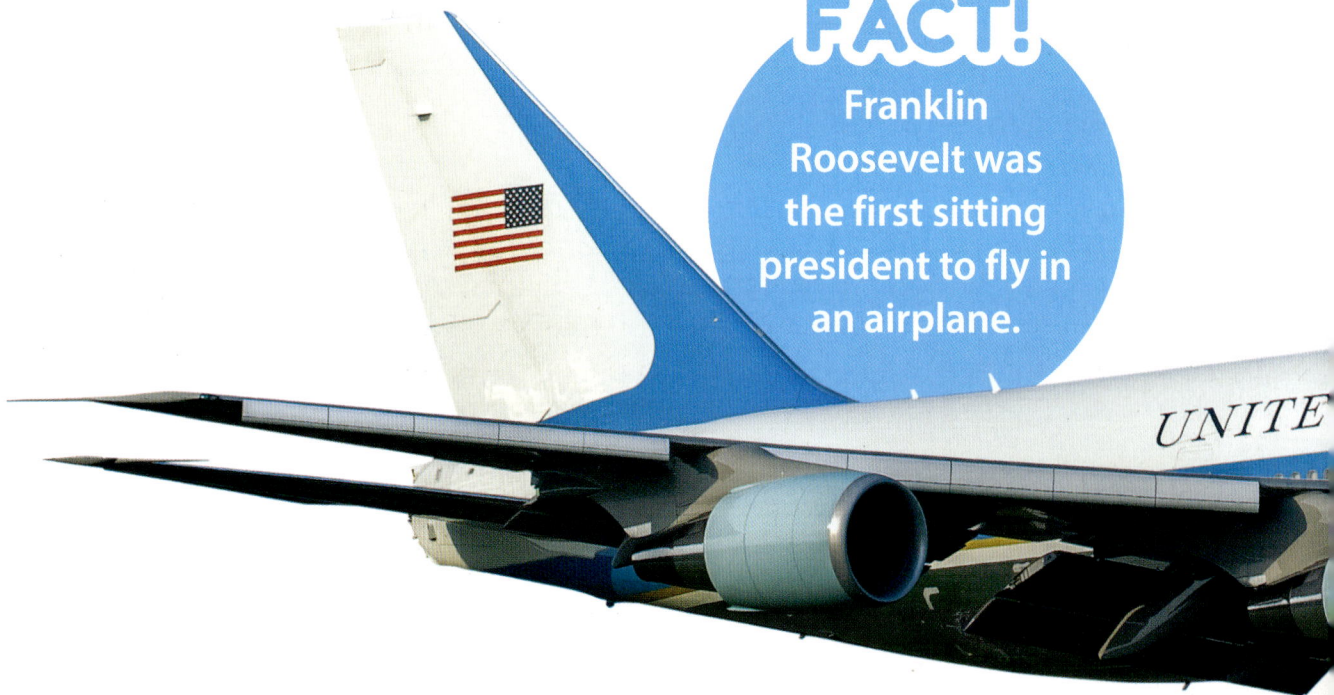

UNITE

There are two kitchens and a dining room. If the president ever gets sick, there is an operating room and a doctor on board.

Size:
231 feet long
(70 m)

How Far:
7,800 miles
(12,553 km)

How High:
45,100 feet
(13,746 m)

How Fast:
600 mph
(966 kmh)

Air Force One is built to keep the president safe. The plane's body is made to stop anything from hitting it. No other planes can fly near it. Every other plane has to fly far away. This plane doesn't have to land to get more fuel. It can get fuel while it flies!

Before the plane lands in a new place, the military lands first. They make sure everything is safe on the ground. There are other things that make Air Force One safe, but they are top secret!

FUN FACT!

Air Force One can serve as a mobile command center for the president.

Boeing

Boeing is a company that makes airplanes. They sell planes to many different airlines that fly them. Boeing planes go all over the world.

One of the biggest Boeing passenger planes is the 747. It was made more than 50 years ago. In 2012, a new 747 was built. It is called the 747-8. It is bigger than the old one. It can carry 700 people!

The smallest Boeing plane is the 737-700. It can carry 150 people.

Boeing 747-8

Size:
232 feet long
(71 m)

How High:
35,000 feet
(10,668 m)

How Far:
9,000 miles
(14,484 km)

How Fast:
614 mph
(988 kmh)

FUN FACT!

The first plane Boeing ever built was a wooden seaplane. It was made in 1916.

Boeing 247

The Boeing 247 was one of the first passenger planes. It was built in 1933 and carried 10 passengers. There were five rows of seats inside. The plane had two propellers. It flew between New York and Los Angeles. The flight took 20 hours! The plane had to stop seven times along the way.

FUN FACT!

In 1934, the Boeing 247 flew from England to Australia! It took almost 93 hours.

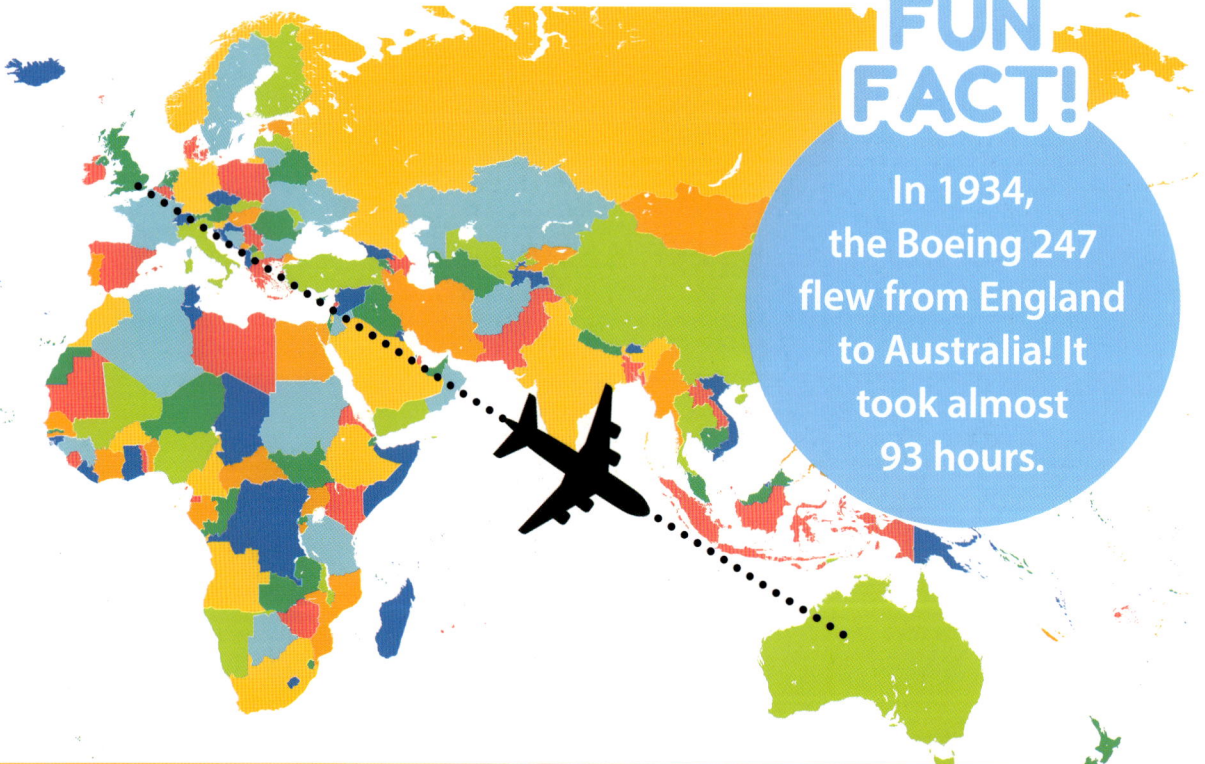

Size:
52 feet long
(16 m)

How High:
24,500 feet
(7,468 m)

How Far:
745 miles
(1,199 km)

How Fast:
200 mph
(322 kmh)

There were 75 Boeing 247 planes built. During World War II, some of the planes were used by the military. They took troops and weapons to where they needed to go.

The Boeing 247 flew until the late 1960s. By then, it only flew during air shows. The Boeing 247 helped people make even better passenger planes.

Did You Know?

There are special rest areas on modern Boeing planes for pilots and crew only. A small room is tucked away in a corner or back of the plane. This is for the flight attendants. There is also a rest area for the pilots near the cockpit.

Concorde

The Concorde could fly from New York to London in less than four hours! It flew passengers from 1976 to 2003. This plane was supersonic. This means it flew faster than sound can travel.

The plane landed on its back tires. It looked almost like a bird landing. The back was curved and it had a pointy nose. The nose moved down so the pilots could see when they were landing.

The Concorde flew faster than Earth can spin!

Size:
204 feet long
(62 m)

How High:
60,000 feet
(18,288 m)

How Far:
4,100 miles
(6,598 km)

How Fast:
1,350 mph
(2,173 kmh)

Since it went so fast, the Concorde got very hot. When things get hot, they can expand. When flying, the plane would grow 8 inches (20 cm) from the heat. This plane had special paint to keep the heat away from the inside.

Did You Know?

The first Concorde plane to fly is now in a museum in France.

The Concorde also had special wings. They were shaped like triangles. This shape is called a delta. The delta shape helped the plane take off smoothly.

Gulfstream G700

The Gulfstream is a small plane. These are sometimes owned by one person or a business, not an airline. They are called private or business jets. The Gulfstream G700 carries 19 passengers.

This plane can reach almost every continent on one tank of fuel. It can also fly very high, even above bad weather.

Did You Know?

The seats inside the Gulfstream move. Passengers can ask for the seats to be moved to where they would like them to be.

The Gulfstream has special lights. The lights copy the sun's light. This helps passengers feel less tired after a long flight.

Size:
110 feet long
(34 m)

How High:
51,000 feet
(15,545 m)

How Far:
8,600 miles
(13,840 km)

How Fast:
700 mph
(1,127 kmh)

FUN FACT!

The Gulfstream has 20 big windows along the cabin of the plane.

Canard

The Canard was the first seaplane. A seaplane is a plane that can land on water. The Canard was built in 1910. That was more than 100 years ago!

The Canard was made to land on the ground at first. In 1911, floats were put on the plane. The plane was put on the Seine River in France to see how well it would float. It sat on top of the water and took off!

Size:
26 feet long
(8 m)

How High:
7 feet
(2 m)

How Far:
1,500 miles
(2,414 km)

How Fast:
56 mph
(90 kmh)

FUN FACT!

The Canard was built by two brothers in France.

Did You Know?

The plane was named Canard, which means "duck" in French.

Cessna Skyhawk 172 Seaplane

The Cessna 172 Skyhawk is small and light. But what makes this plane special? It is made to take off and land on the ground or the water.

Size:
27 feet long
(8 m)

How High:
14,000 feet
(4,267 m)

How Far:
730 miles
(1,175 km)

How Fast:
188 mph
(303 kmh)

FUN FACT!

More Cessna 172 planes have been made than any other plane ever.

When it needs to be on water, floats are added to the plane. When the seaplane is ready for takeoff, the pilot slowly drives it down a ramp. It goes into the water and floats. The pilot gets the plane in place. It moves forward, going faster and faster. Then up it goes!

G21A Grumman Goose

The Grumman Goose was a flying boat. At first, it was a passenger plane. It became a military plane during World War II. It also flew for the coast guard.

Size:
39 feet
(12 m) long

How Far:
736 miles
(1,184 km)

How High:
21,300 feet
(6,492 m)

How Fast:
191 mph
(307 kmh)

Did You Know?

The coast guard patrols the lakes, rivers, and oceans around the United States. They protect people and the environment. Part of their job is rescuing people at sea. They also help out after big storms.

The bottom of the Goose was curved. It looked like a boat. It also had built-in floats below each wing to help it sit on the water. The tires on the plane sat inside the sides of the plane. They came out when the plane needed to land on the ground.

FUN FACT!

During World War II, the Goose was used to rescue soldiers at sea.

OS2U Kingfisher Floatplane

Most planes take off from a runway. The Kingfisher floatplane took off from a ship! It was launched using a catapult when it was ready to take off. When it was time to get back on the ship, a crane lifted the plane out of the water.

Did You Know?

Like the Kingfisher floatplane, the kingfisher bird is very good at swooping down to the surface of the water. But the bird's job is to catch fish.

Size:
34 feet long
(10 m)

How High:
13,000 feet
(3,962 m)

How Far:
805 miles
(1,296 km)

How Fast:
164 mph
(264 kmh)

FUN FACT!
The Kingfisher was an ambulance in the air.

The plane flew during World War II. It made lots of flights over the Pacific Ocean. It rescued people. It had a place where people could lie down if they were hurt.

Cessna 170

It's not easy for a regular plane to land in snow. All the snow has to be taken away first. The Cessna 170 is different. This plane has wheels, but when it needs to land in snow, it puts on skis!

FUN FACT!

Ski planes do not have brakes.

Size:
25 feet long
(8 m)

How Far:
592 miles
(953 km)

How High:
15,500 feet
(4,724 m)

How Fast:
160 mph
(257 kmh)

The pilot has to know how deep the snow is before landing. A plane can sink if it lands in a deep spot. Pilots also have to stay away from water and ice. They can be slippery!

Extra 330SC

This plane is made for air shows. People watch from the ground as the plane flies all over. It is light and fast. It can spin and go upside down. It also dives quickly. The Extra 330SC performs tricks called aerobatics.

Did You Know?

Aerobatics were taught as a way to quickly get away from enemy planes during World War I. Now they are done for fun!

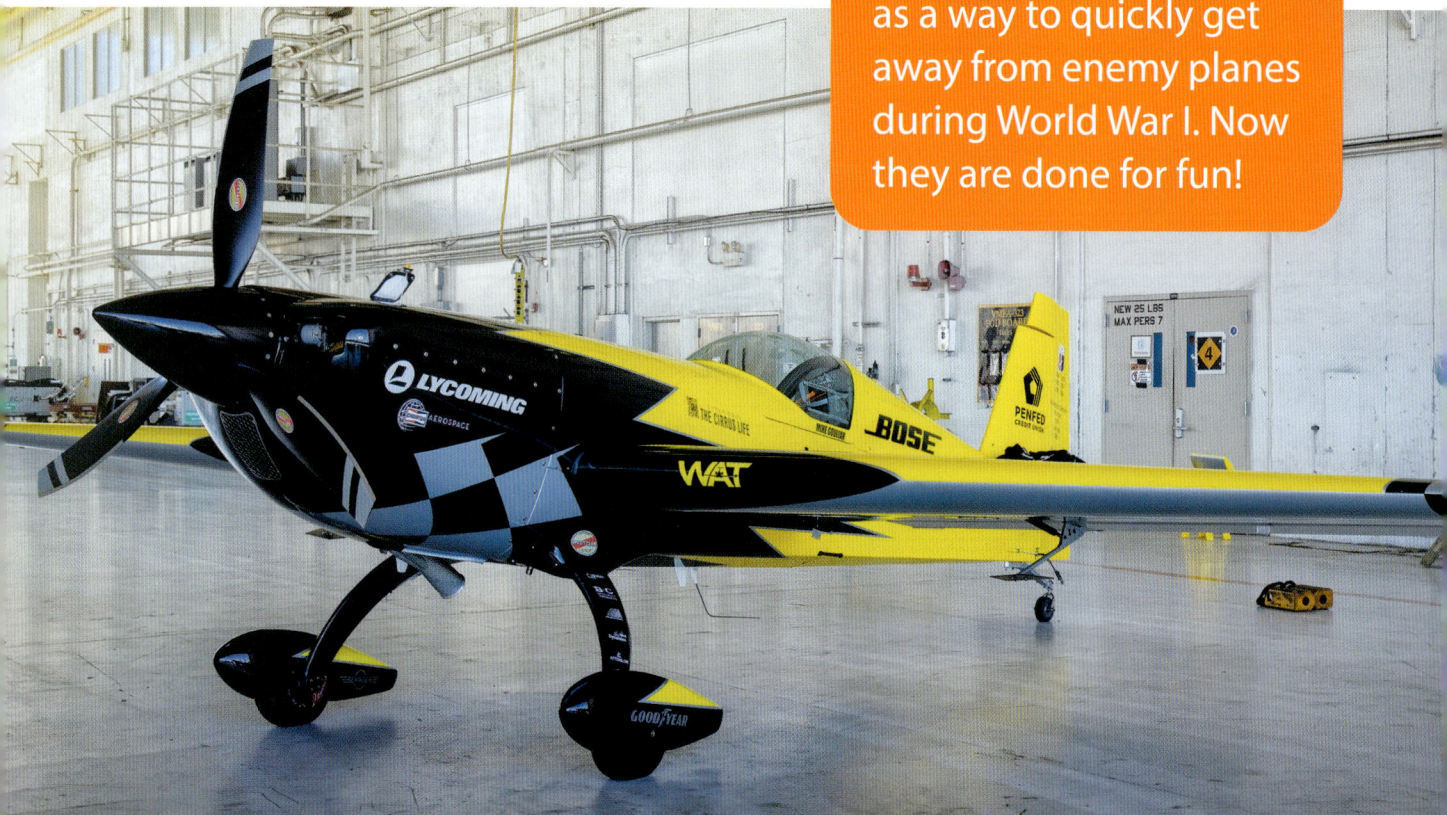

FUN FACT!

These planes are meant to fly for only about 20 minutes at a time.

Size:
22 feet long
(7 m)

How High:
16,000 feet
(4,877 m)

How Far:
373 miles
(600 km)

How Fast:
230 mph
(370 kmh)

There is room for one pilot on the plane. The plane is small but powerful. Pilots have to be skilled at flying it.

Gee Bee

The Gee Bee was a fast plane built for air shows. The plane was made by a family of brothers. They wanted to be part of an air show in Ohio. The show was a competition for the best plane.

FUN FACT!

The Gee Bees got their name from the initials of the people who built the plane: the Grantville brothers.

Size:
18 feet long
(5 m)

How High:
15,000 feet
(4,572 m)

How Far:
630 miles
(1,014 km)

How Fast:
309 mph
(497 kmh)

Gee Bee

1997

32 USA

Did You Know?

Air shows have been popular events for a long time. They are still popular today. People watch as planes show off their aerobatics. Military planes are sometimes in shows too.

The Gee Bee flew in lots of shows. It won many airplane races too. Gee Bees were very colorful and stood out in the air. Some were red. Others were yellow. An image of this colorful plane was once put on a postage stamp!

Solar Impulse 2

In 2016, the Solar Impulse 2 was the first plane to fly around the world using the sun's energy. The trip took more than one year. The plane made about 15 stops along the way. There were two pilots, but there was room on the plane for only one. The pilots took turns flying the plane.

Size:
71 feet long
(22 m)

How Far:
21,800 miles
(35,084 km)

How High:
30,000 feet
(9,144 m)

How Fast:
43 mph
(69 kmh)

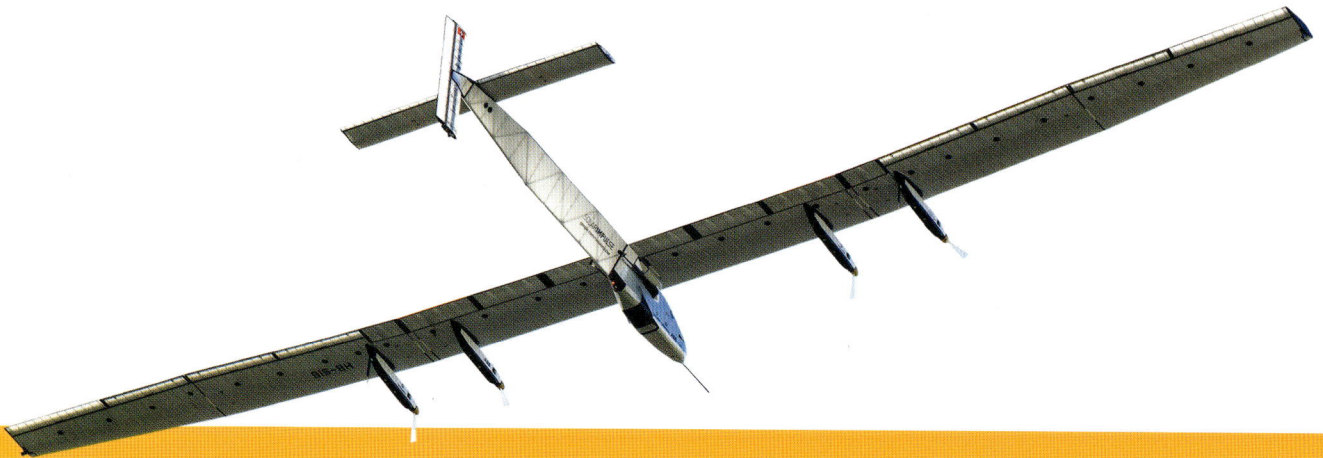

Did You Know?

The plane uses battery power at night. Why? Because it cannot get energy from the sun in the dark!

The Solar Impulse 2 has long wings. It also has lots of solar panels. The panels catch the sun's energy. Some of the energy goes to batteries inside the plane.

SpaceShipTwo

SpaceShipTwo was made to take people to space! It is not ready yet, but it will be ready soon. The plane has made some test flights to make sure it can reach space safely. The first one was in 2018. SpaceShipTwo flew high enough to exit Earth's atmosphere and touch space.

Size:
60 feet long
(18 m)

How High:
361,000 feet
(110,033 m)

How Far:
62 miles
(100 km)

How Fast:
2,500 mph
(4,023 kmh)

FUN FACT!
When the plane is ready, it will fit six passengers and two pilots.

The plane has a rocket engine. This helps it get high in the air. Passengers will have to train for three days to get ready for the flight. This is because the flight is fast. And in space, there is no gravity. Everyone will float!

SpaceShipTwo won't take off from the ground. Instead, it will attach to a bigger plane. The carrier plane will fly high into the sky. SpaceShipTwo will drop off and go higher. The flight will take almost three hours.

Once passengers reach space, they will be able to see for 1,000 miles (1,609 km) in all directions. That's about the distance from Washington, DC, to Des Moines, Iowa!

Did You Know?

White Knight Two is a special aircraft that carries SpaceShipTwo into the air. The SpaceShipTwo rides in the middle.

Air Tractor AT-802F

The Air Tractor helps fight fires. It is nicknamed "Fire Boss." The pilots take the plane over a fire. They use a controller to dump water on the fire. This plane needs to fly low so water can reach the fire.

Size:
36 feet long
(11 m)

How High:
8,000 feet
(2,438 m)

How Far:
800 miles
(1,287 km)

How Fast:
221 mph
(356 kmh)

FUN FACT!

It can dump 14,000 gallons (52,996 L) of water over a fire in one hour!

The water is kept in a tank on the plane. If there is a lake or river close by, the Air Tractor can scoop up water if needed. The Air Tractor can hold 820 gallons (3,104 L) of water. That's the same as 820 jugs of milk!

C-20A Environmental Science Research Aircraft

This NASA jet is a science lab in the air. The inside of the plane does not have a lot of seats. Instead, it has equipment, or tools, to help scientists study Earth.

Size:
83 feet long
(25 m)

How High:
45,000 feet
(13,716 m)

How Far:
3,900 miles
(6,276 km)

How Fast:
529 mph
(851 kmh)

Did You Know?

This plane helps scientists track changes to Earth's surface during and after a volcano.

The plane carries a radar system. Radar collects information from what it sees on the ground. It can track wildfires to see how much land is burning. Radar can also measure parts of Earth's surface. This helps scientists learn about the land and earthquakes.

Crop Dusters

Some planes help farmers with their crops. That's what the Grumman G-164 Ag-Cat did. It was a plane called a crop duster. It was the first plane built to be used on farms.

Crop dusters are still used today. The pilot flies the plane over a field, and the plane sprays crops with pesticides. Pesticides keep bugs away from crops.

Size:
23 feet long
(7 m)

How High:
13,000 feet
(3,962 m)

How Far:
281 miles
(452 km)

How Fast:
147 mph
(237 kmh)

FUN FACT!

A crop duster helps farmers save time. It can spray crops faster than a tractor on land.

Crop dusters need to fly low so the spray can reach the crops. There are sprayers under each wing. The pilot controls when the spray comes out.

FAAM Airborne Laboratory

This plane is also called the Flying Laboratory. It is a science lab in the air. It is used to study Earth's air, clouds, and weather.

Size:
102 feet long
(31 m)

How High:
35,000 feet
(10,668 m)

How Far:
2,100 miles
(3,380 km)

How Fast:
464 mph
(747 kmh)

There are lots of computers inside the plane. They sit on desks that are stuck to the floor. This way, the computers do not move when the plane is flying.

The nose of the plane has a special tool. It measures the wind outside the plane.

WORKING PLANES

The Flying Laboratory flies all over the world. Scientists learn about air pollution, climate change, and weather from different places.

Earth's climate has been changing. Many places are getting warmer. This can cause problems, like more storms and hurricanes. Air pollution is something that makes Earth warmer.

The Flying Laboratory gathers information. Scientists use it to find ways to help the environment. Many people are working hard to help make climate change better.

FUN FACT!

When the Flying Lab is over the ocean, it can fly as low as 50 feet (15 m).

Water Scooper

A water scooper is a plane that picks up water while flying. The plane flies close to a lake, ocean, and sometimes a river. It scoops water into a tank at the bottom of the plane. The plane dumps water over the flames to put out the fire.

Did You Know?

Water scoopers drop water on fires from 100 feet (30 m) in the air.

Size:
70 feet long
(21 m)

How Far:
1,520 miles
(2,446 km)

How High:
20,000 feet
(6,096 m)

How Fast:
200 mph
(322 kmh)

One of the best water scoopers is the Bombardier 415. It can scoop 680 gallons (2,574 L) in one pass! It is called a Super Scooper!

Weatherbird WC-130J

One of the Weatherbird's main jobs is to fly into hurricanes! It also flies into winter storms. The plane gathers information. This helps scientists learn more about storms: how they work, how they move, and how big they are.

Size:
90 feet long
(27 m)

How High:
26,000 feet
(7,925 m)

How Far:
1,800 miles
(2,897 km)

How Fast:
417 mph
(671 kmh)

The plane can stay in the air for almost 18 hours. Only five people at a time can fly on the big plane. Two are pilots. The other three study the weather.

WORKING PLANES

The inside of the Weatherbird has lots of tools. But one special tool is dropped out of the plane! It is called a dropsonde.

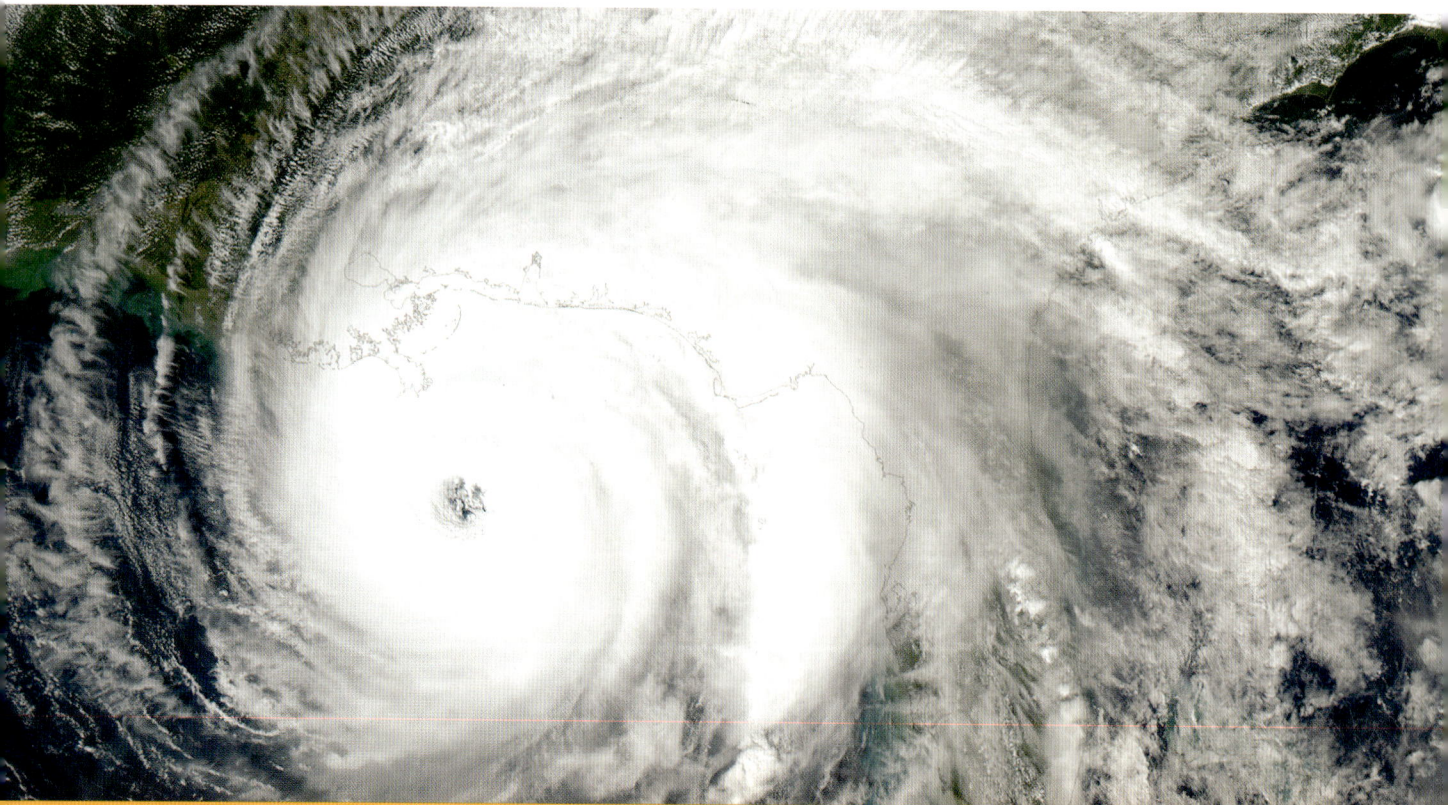

The dropsonde falls into the eye of a hurricane. The eye is the center of the storm. The dropsonde records things about the hurricane as it falls. It sends everything it learns back to the plane.

The dropsonde has a parachute. This lets it land smoothly back on the ground.

FUN FACT!

The people who fly in the Weatherbird are sometimes called hurricane hunters.

GLOSSARY

aerobatics
Special flying tricks such as rolling, diving, and spinning.

cargo
Goods that are moved in an airplane or other vehicle, such as a truck.

catapult
A machine used to fling heavy objects very far into the air.

jumbo jet
A huge airplane that can carry lots of people.

laboratory
A place where scientists do experiments.

navigator
A person who helps others find their way.

parachutes
Large, light fabrics that are used to slow down people or objects falling to the ground.

passenger
A person who rides in a vehicle, such as an airplane or car.

pollution
When the environment is made dirty by chemicals, gases, or other harmful things.

propeller
Blades on the front of wings of some planes that spin very fast to help the plane fly.

stealth
Something that is hard to find.

TO LEARN MORE

More Books to Read

Amstutz, Lisa J. *Airplanes.* Focus Readers, 2018

Camellia, Mavis. *We Are Going on an Airplane.* Little Book Wallah, 2022.

Holzweiss, Kristina A. *My First Book of Airplanes.* Rockridge Press, 2022.

Online Resources

Booklinks
NONFICTION NETWORK
FREE! ONLINE NONFICTION RESOURCES

To learn more about planes, please visit **abdobooklinks.com** or scan this QR code. These links are routinely monitored and updated to provide the most current information available.

INDEX

PHOTO CREDITS

cvjc